CHRISTIANITY AND PATRIOTISM

CHRISTIANITY AND PATRIOTISM

LEO TOLSTOY

Translated from the Original Russian and Edited by

LEO WIENER

*Assistant Professor of Slavic Languages
at Harvard University*

A TOLSTOY BOOK

A TOLSTOY BOOK

Published by Wildside Press LLC.
www.wildsidebooks.com

AUTHORS NOTE

The Franco-Russian celebrations which took place in France, in the month of October of last year, provoked in me, as no doubt in many other people, at first a feeling of amusement, then of perplexity, and at last of indignation, which I intended to express in a short article in a periodical; but, the more I dwelt on the chief causes of this strange phenomenon, the more did I arrive at the considerations which I now offer to my readers.

I.

Russians and Frenchmen have lived for many centuries, knowing one another, entering with one another at times into friendly, more often, I am sorry to say, into very hostile relations, which have been provoked by their governments; suddenly, because two years ago a French squadron arrived at Kronstadt, and the officers of the squadron, upon landing, ate and drank a lot of wine in various places, hearing and uttering upon these occasions many lying and stupid words, and because, in the year 1893, a similar Russian squadron arrived at Toulon, and the officers of the Russian squadron ate and drank a lot in Paris, hearing and uttering upon that occasion more lying and stupid words than before, it happened that not only the men who ate, drank, and talked, but even those who were present, and even those who were not present, but only heard and read of it in newspapers, all these millions of Russians and Frenchmen suddenly imagined that they somehow were particularly in love with one another, that is, that all the French loved all the Russians, and all the Russians loved all the French.

These sentiments were last October expressed in France in a most unusual manner.

Here is the way the reception of the Russian sailors is described in the *Rural Messenger*, a newspaper which collects its information from all the others:

"At the meeting of the Russian and French vessels, both, besides the salvos of guns, greeted one another with hearty, ecstatic shouts, 'Hurrah,' 'Long live Russia,' 'Long live France!'

"These were joined by bands of music (which came on many private steamers), playing the Russian hymn, 'God save the Tsar,' and the French Marseillaise; the public on the private vessels waved their hats, flags, handkerchiefs, and bouquets; on many barques there were peasants with their wives and children, and they all had bouquets in their hands, and even the children waved the bouquets and shouted at the top of their voices, 'Vive la Russie!' Our sailors, upon seeing such national transport, were unable to restrain their tears....

"In the harbour all the ships-of-war which were then at Toulon were drawn out in two lines, and our squadron passed between them; in front was the ironclad of the admiralty, and this was followed by the rest. There ensued a most solemn minute.

"On the Russian ironclad, fifteen salvos were fired in honour of the French squadron, and a French ironclad replied with double the number, with thirty salvos. From the French vessels thundered the sounds of the Russian hymn. The French sailors climbed up on the sail-yards and masts; loud exclamations of greeting proceeded uninterruptedly from the two squadrons and from the private vessels; the caps of the sailors, the hats and handkerchiefs of the public,—all were thrown up triumphantly in honour of the dear guests. On all sides, on the water and on the shore, there boomed one common call, 'Long live Russia! Long live France!'

"In conformity with naval law, Admiral Avelán and the officers of his staff landed, in order to greet the local authorities. On the quay the Russian sailors were met by the chief marine staff of France and the superior officers of the port of Toulon. There ensued a universal friendly hand-shaking, accompanied by the boom of cannon and the ringing of bells. A band of marine music played the hymn 'God save the Tsar,' drowned by the thunderous shouts of the public, 'Long live the Tsar! Long live Russia!' These exclamations blended into one mighty sound, which drowned the music and the salvos from the guns.

"Eye-witnesses declare that at this moment the enthusiasm of the innumerable mass of people reached its highest limits, and that it is impossible to express in words with what sensations the hearts of all those present were filled. Admiral Avelán, with bared head, and accompanied by Russian and French officers, directed his steps to the building of the Marine Office, where the French minister of marine was waiting for him.

"In receiving the admiral, the minister said: 'Kronstadt and Toulon are two places which bear witness to the sympathy between the Russian and the French nations; you will everywhere be met as dear friends. The government and all of France welcome you upon your arrival and that of your companions, who represent a great and noble nation.'

"The admiral replied that he was not able to express all his gratitude. 'The Russian squadron and all of Russia,' he said, 'will remember the reception you have given us.'

"After a short conversation, the admiral, saying good-bye to the minister, a second time thanked him for the reception, and added, 'I do not want to part from you before pronouncing those words which are imprinted in all Russian hearts: "Long live France!"'" (*Rural Messenger*, 1893, No. 41.)

Such was the meeting at Toulon. In Paris the meeting and the celebrations were more remarkable still.

Here is the way the meeting in Paris was described in the newspapers: "All eyes were directed to the Boulevard des Italiens, whence the Russian sailors were to appear. Finally the boom of a whole hurricane of exclamations and applauses is heard in the distance. The boom grows stronger and more audible. The hurricane is apparently approaching. A mighty motion takes place on the square. Policemen rush forward to clear a path toward the Cercle Militaire, but this is by no means an easy task. There is an incredible crush and pressure in the crowd.... Finally the head of the procession appears in the square. At the same moment a deafening shout, 'Vive la Russie! Vive les Russes!' rises over it. All bare their heads, the public, packed close in the windows, on the balconies, perched even on the roofs, wave handkerchiefs, flags, and hats, applaud madly, and from the windows of the upper stories throw clouds of small many-coloured cockades. A whole sea of handkerchiefs, hats, and flags surges above the heads of the crowd in the square: 'Vive la Russie! Vive les Russes!' shouts this mass of one hundred thousand people, trying to get a look at the dear guests, extending their hands to them, and in every way expressing their sympathies" (*New Time*).

Another correspondent writes that the transport of the crowd bordered on delirium. A Russian publicist, who was in Paris at that time, describes this entrance of the sailors in the following manner: "They tell the truth,—it was an incident of world-wide import, wondrous, touching, soul-stirring, making the heart quiver with that love which discerns the brothers in men, and which detests bloodshed and concomitant acts of violence, the tearing away of the children from their beloved mother. I have been in some kind of an intoxication for several hours.

I felt so strange, and even so weak, as I stood at the station of the Lyons Railway, among the representatives of the French administration in their gold-embroidered uniforms, among the members of the municipality in full dress, and heard the shouts, 'Vive la Russie! Vive le Czar!' and our national hymn, which was played several times in succession. Where am I? What has happened? What magic stream has united all this into one feeling, into one mind? Does one not feel here the presence of the God of love and brotherhood, the presence of something higher, something ideal, which descends upon men only in lofty moments? The heart is so full of something beautiful and pure and exalted, that the pen is not able to express it all. Words pale before what I saw, what I felt. It is not transport,—the word is too banal,—it is something better than transport. It is more picturesque, profounder, more joyous, more varied. It is impossible to describe what happened at the Cercle Militaire, when Admiral Avelán appeared on the balcony of a second story. Words will not tell anything here. During the Te Deum, when the choristers sang in the church 'Save, O Lord, thy people,' there burst through the open door the solemn sounds of the Marseillaise, which was played in the street by an orchestra of wind-instruments. There was something astounding and inexpressible in the impression conveyed" (*New Time*, October, 1893).

II.

After arriving in France, the Russian sailors for two weeks went from one celebration to another, and in the middle or at the end of every celebration they ate, drank, and talked; and the information as to what they ate and drank on Wednesday and where and what on Friday, and what was said upon that occasion, was wired home and conveyed to the whole of Russia. The moment some Russian captain drank the health of France, this at once became known to the whole world, and the moment the Russian admiral said, "I drink to fair France!" these words were immediately borne over the whole world. But more than that: the scrupulousness of the newspapers was such that they reported not only the toasts, but even many dinners, with the cakes and appetizers which were used at these dinners.

Thus it said in one issue of a newspaper that the dinner was "an artistic production:"

> "Consommé de volailles, petits pâtés
> Mousse de hommard parisienne
> Noisette de bœuf à la béarnaise
> Faisans à la Périgord
> Casseroles de truffes au champagne
> Chaufroid de volailles à la Toulouse
> Salade russe
> Croute de fruits toulonaise
> Parfait à l'ananas
> Desserts"

In the next number it said:

"In a culinary sense the dinner left nothing to be desired. The menu consisted of the following:

"Potage livonien et St. Germain
Zéphyrs Nantua
Esturgeon braisé moldave
Selle de daguet grand veneur,"

and so forth.

The next number described another menu. With every menu a detailed description was given of the wines which the fêted men consumed,—such and such "voodka" such and such Bourgogne vieux, Grand Moët, and so forth. In an English paper there was an account of all the intoxicants consumed by the celebrators. This amount is so enormous that it is doubtful if all the drunkards of Russia and of France could have drunk so much in so short a time.

They reported also the speeches which were made by the celebrators, but the menus were more varied than the speeches. The speeches consisted invariably of the same words in all kinds of combinations and permutations. The meaning of these words was always one and the same: "We love one another tenderly, we are in transport, because we have so suddenly fallen in love with one another. Our aim is not war and not revanche, and not the return of provinces taken, but only *peace*, the benefaction of *peace*, the security of *peace*, the rest and *peace* of Europe. Long live the Emperor of Russia and the empress,—we love them and we love *peace*. Long live the president of the republic and his wife,—we love them, too, and we love *peace*. Long live France, Russia, their fleets, and their armies. We love the army, too, and *peace*, and the chief of the squadron." The speeches generally ended, as in couplets, with the words, "Toulon, Kronstadt," or "Kronstadt, Toulon." And the names of these places, where so much food was eaten and so many kinds of wine were consumed, were pronounced like words reminding one of the loftiest, most valorous of acts of the representatives of both nations, words after which there was nothing else to be said, because everything was comprehensible. "We love one another, and we love peace. Kronstadt, Toulon!" What else can be added to this? Especially with the accompaniment of solemn music, playing simultaneously two hymns, one—praising the Tsar and asking God for all kinds of benefactions for him, and the other—cursing all kings and promising their ruin.

The men who expressed their sentiments of love particularly well received decorations and rewards; other men for the same services, or simply out of a superabundance of feelings, were given the strangest and most unexpected presents,—thus the Emperor of Russia received from the French squadron some kind of a golden book, in which, I think, nothing was written, and if there was, it was something that nobody needed to know, and the chief of the Russian squadron received, among other presents, a still more remarkable object, an aluminum plough, covered with flowers, and many other just as unexpected presents.

Besides, all these strange acts were accompanied by still stranger religious ceremonies and public prayers, which, it would seem, the French had long ago outlived. Since the days of the Concordat there had hardly been offered so many prayers as in that short time. All the French suddenly became unusually pious, and carefully hung up in the rooms of the Russian sailors those very images which they had just as carefully removed from their schools, as being harmful tools of superstition, and they kept praying all the time. Cardinals and bishops everywhere prescribed prayers, and themselves prayed, uttering the strangest prayers. Thus the Bishop of Toulon at the launching of the ironclad *Joriguiberi* prayed to the God of peace, making people feel, however, that, if it came to a pinch, he could address also the God of war.

"What her fate will be," said the bishop, in reference to the ironclad, "God alone knows. No one knows whether she will belch forth death from her appalling bosom. But if, invoking now the God of peace, we should later have occasion to invoke the God of war, we are firmly convinced that the *Joriguiberi* will go forth side by side with the mighty boats whose crews have this day entered into such a close fraternal union with our own. Far from us be such a prospect, and may the present festivity leave nothing but a peaceful recollection, like the recollection of the *Grand Duke Constantine*, which was present here (in 1857) at the launching of the ship *Quirinal*, and may the friendship of France and of Russia make these two nations the guardians of peace."

In the meantime tens of thousands of telegrams flew from Russia to France, and from France to Russia. French women greeted Russian women. Russian women expressed their gratitude to the French women. A troupe of Russian actors greeted some French actors, and the French actors informed them that they harboured deeply in their hearts the greeting of the Russian actors. Some Russian candidates for judicial positions, who served in a Circuit Court of some town or other, expressed their enthusiasm for the French nation. General So and So thanked Madame So and So, and Madame So and So assured General So and So of her sentiments for the Russian nation; Russian children wrote verses of welcome to French children, and the French children answered in verse and in prose; the Russian minister of education assured the French minister of education of the sentiments of sudden love for the French, which were experienced by all the children, scholars, and authors subject to his ministry; members of a society for the protection of animals expressed their ardent attachment for the French, and so did the Council of the City of Kazán.

The canon of the eparchy of Arras informed his Worship, the chief priest of the Russian court clergy, that he could affirm that deep in the hearts of all the French cardinals and archbishops there was imprinted a love for Russia and his Majesty Alexander III. and his most august family, and that the Russian and French clergy professed almost the selfsame religion and equally honoured the Virgin; to which his Worship, the chief priest, replied that the prayers of the French clergy for the most august family reëchoed joyfully in the hearts of the whole Russian Tsar-loving family, and that, since the Russian people also worshipped the Holy Virgin, it could count on France in life and in death. Almost the same information was vouchsafed by different generals, telegraph operators, and dealers in groceries. Everybody congratulated somebody on something and thanked somebody for something.

The excitement was so great that the most unusual acts were committed, but no one observed their unusual character, and all, on the contrary, approved of them, went into ecstasies over them, and, as though fearing lest they should be too late, hastened to commit similar acts, so as not to fall behind the rest. If protests were expressed in words and in writing and in printing against these mad acts, pointing out their irrationality, such protests were concealed or squelched.

To say nothing of all the millions of work-days which were wasted on these festivities, of the wholesale drunkenness of all the participants, which was encouraged by all the powers, to say nothing of the insipidity of the speeches made, the maddest and most cruel things were done, and no one paid any attention to them.

Thus several dozens of men were crushed to death, and no one found it necessary to mention this fact. One correspondent wrote that a Frenchman told him at a ball that now there could hardly be found a woman in Paris who would not be false to her duties, in order to satisfy the wishes of some Russian sailor—and all this passed by unnoticed, as something that ought to be. There occurred cases of distinct madness. Thus one woman, dressing herself in a garment of the colours of the Franco-Russian flags, waited for the sailors and, exclaiming, "Vive la Russie!" jumped from the bridge into the river and was drowned.

Women in general played in these festivities a prominent part and even guided the men. Besides throwing flowers and all kinds of ribbons, and offering presents and addresses, French women made for the Russian sailors and kissed them; some of them for some reason brought their children to them, to be kissed by them, and when the Russian sailors complied with their wish, all persons present went into ecstasies and wept.

This strange excitement was so infectious that, as one correspondent tells, an apparently absolutely sound Russian sailor, after two days of contemplation of what took place around him, in the middle of the day jumped from the ship into the sea and, swimming, shouted, "Vive la France!" When he was taken aboard and asked why he had done so, he replied that he had made a vow that in honour of France he would swim around the ship.

Thus the undisturbed excitement grew and grew, like a ball of rolling wet snow, and finally reached such dimensions that not only the persons present, not only predisposed, weak-nerved, but even strong, normal men fell a prey to the general mood and became abnormally affected.

I remember how I, absent-mindedly reading one of these descriptions of the solemnity of the reception of the sailors, suddenly felt a feeling, akin to meekness of spirit, even a readiness for tears, communicated to me, so that I had to make an effort to overcome this feeling.

III.

Lately Sikórski, a professor of psychiatry, described in the *Kíev University Record* the psychopathic epidemic, as he calls it, of the Malévannians, as manifested in a few villages of Vasilkóv County of the Government of Kíev. The essence of this epidemic, as Mr. Sikórski, the investigator of it, says, consisted in this, that certain persons of these villages, under the influence of their leader, by the name of Malévanny, came to imagine that the end of the world was at hand, and so, changing their whole mode of life, began to distribute their property, to dress up, and to eat savoury food, and stopped working. The professor found the condition of these men to be abnormal. He says: "Their unusual good nature frequently passed into exaltation, a joyous condition, which was devoid of external motives. They were sentimentally disposed: excessively polite, talkative, mobile, with tears of joy appearing easily and just as easily disappearing. They sold their necessaries, in order to provide themselves with umbrellas, silk kerchiefs, and similar objects, and at that the kerchiefs served them only as ornaments for their toilet. They ate many sweet things. They were always in a cheerful mood, and they led an idle life,—visited one another, walked together.... When the obviously absurd character of their refusal to work was pointed out to them, one every time heard in reply the stereotyped phrase, 'If I want to, I shall work, and if I do not want to, why should I compel myself?'"

The learned professor considers the condition of these men a pronounced case of a psychopathic epidemic, and, advising the government to take certain measures against its spread, ends his communication with the words: "Malévannism is the wail of a morbidly sick population and a supplication to be freed from liquor and to have education and sanitary conditions improved."

But if Malévannism is the wail of a morbidly sick population and a supplication to be freed from liquor and from harmful social conditions, then this new disease, which has appeared in Paris and has with alarming rapidity embraced a great part of the city population of France and almost the whole of governmental and cultured Russia, is just such an alarming wail of a morbid population and just such a supplication to be freed from liquor and from false social conditions.

And if we must admit that the psychopathic suffering of Malévannism is dangerous, and that the government has done well to follow the professor's advice and remove the leaders of Malévannism by confining some of them in lunatic asylums and monasteries and by deporting others to distant places, how much more dangerous must be considered to be this new epidemic, which appeared in Toulon and Paris and from there spread over the whole of France and of Russia, and how much more necessary it is, if not for the government, at least for society, to take decisive measures against the spread of such epidemics!

The resemblance between the diseases is complete. There is the same good nature, passing into causeless and joyful exaltation, the same sentimentality, excessive politeness, talkativeness, the same constant tears of meekness of spirit, which come and go without cause, the same festive mood, the same walking for pleasure and visiting one another, the same dressing up in the best clothes, the same proneness for sweet food, the same senseless talks, the same idleness, the same singing and music, the same leadership of the women, and the same clownish phase of attitudes passionelles, which Mr. Sikórski has noticed in the case of the Malévannians; that is, as I understand this word, those different, unnatural poses, which men assume during solemn meetings, receptions, and after-dinner speeches.

The resemblance is complete. The only difference is this,—and the difference is very great for the society in which these phenomena are taking place,—that there it is the aberration of a few dozen peaceful, poor village people, who live on their small means and, therefore, cannot exert any violence on their neighbours, and who infect others only by the personal and oral transmission of their mood, while here it is the aberration of millions of people, who possess enormous sums of money and means for exerting violence against other people,—guns, bayonets, fortresses, ironclads, melinite, dynamite, and who, besides, have at their command the most energetic means for the dissemination of their madness, the post, the telegraph, an enormous number of newspapers, and all kinds of publications, which are printed without cessation and carry the infection to all the corners of the globe. There is also this difference, that the first not only do not get themselves drunk, but even do not use any intoxicating liquor, while the second are constantly in a state of semi-intoxication, which they never stop maintaining in themselves. And so for a society in which these phenomena are taking place, there is the same difference between the Kíev epidemic, during which, according to Mr. Sikórski's information, it does not appear that they commit any violence or murders, and the one which made its appearance in Paris, where in one procession twenty women were crushed to death, as there is between a piece of coal, which has leaped out of the stove and is glowing on the floor without igniting it, and a fire which is already enveloping the door and walls of the house. In the worst case the consequences of the Kíev epidemic will consist in this, that the peasants of one millionth part of Russia will spend what they have earned by hard labour, and will be unable to pay the Crown taxes; but the consequences from the Toulon-Paris epidemic, which is embracing men who are in possession of a terrible power, of vast sums of money, and of implements of violence and of the dissemination of their madness, can and must be terrible.

IV.

We can with pity listen to the delirium of a feeble, de-fenceless, crazy old man, in his cap and cloak, and even not contradict him, and even jestingly agree with him; but when it is a whole crowd of sound insane people, who have broken away from their confinement, and these people bristle from head to foot with sharp daggers, swords, and loaded revolvers, and madly flourish these death-dealing weapons, we can no longer agree with them, and we cannot be at rest even for a minute. The same is true of that condition of excitement, provoked by the French celebrations, in which Russian and French society finds itself at the present time.

It is true, in all the speeches, in all the toasts, pro-nounced at these celebrations, in all the articles concern-ing these celebrations, they never stopped talking of the importance of everything which was taking place for the guarantee of peace. Even the advocates of war did not speak of hatred of those who snatch away provinces, but of some kind of a love which somehow hates.

But we know of the slyness of all men who are men-tally diseased, and it is this most persistent repetition of our not wanting war, but peace, and the reticence regard-ing that of which all think, that form a most menacing phenomenon.

In answering a toast at a dinner given in the Palace of the Elysées, the Russian ambassador said: "Before drinking a toast to which will respond from the depth of their hearts, not only those who are within these walls, but even those—and, that, too, with equal force—whose hearts near by and far away, at all the points of great, fair France, as also in all of Russia, at the present moment are beating in unison with ours,—permit me to offer to you the expression of our profoundest gratitude for the words of welcome which were addressed by you to our admiral, whom our Tsar has charged with the mission of paying back your visit at Kronstadt. Considering the high importance which you enjoy, your words characterize the true significance of the magnificent *peaceful* festivities, which are celebrated with such wonderful unanimity, loyalty, and sincerity."

The same unjustifiable mention of peace is found in the speech of the French president: "The ties of love, which unite Russia and France," he said, "and which two years ago were strengthened by touching manifestations, of which our fleet was the object at Kronstadt, become tighter and tighter with every day, and the honourable exchange of our amicable sentiments must inspire all those who take to heart the benefactions of peace, confidence, and security," and so forth.

Both speeches quite unexpectedly and without any cause refer to the benefactions of peace and to peaceful celebrations.

The same occurs in the telegrams which were exchanged between the Emperor of Russia and the President of France. The Emperor of Russia telegraphed:

"Au moment où l'escadre russe quitte la France, il me tient à cœur de vous exprimer combien je suis touché et reconnaissant de l'accueil chaleureux et splendide, que mes marins ont trouvé partout sur le sol français. Les témoignages de vive sympathie qui se sont manifestés encore une fois avec tant d'éloquence, joindront un nouveau lien à ceux qui unissent les deux pays et contribueront, je l'espère, à l'affermissement de la paix générale, objet de leurs efforts et de leurs vœux les plus constants," etc.

The President of France in his reply telegraphed as follows:

"La dépêche dont je remercie votre Majesté m'est parvenue au moment ou je quittais Toulon pour rentrer à Paris. La belle escadre sur laquelle j'ai eu la vive satisfaction de saluer le pavillon russe dans les eaux françaises, l'accueil cordial et spontané que vos braves marins ont rencontré partout en France affirment une fois de plus avec éclat les sympathies sincères qui unissent nos deux pays. Ils marquent en même temps une foi profonde dans l'influence bienfaisante que peuvent exercer ensemble deux grandes nations devouées à la cause de la paix."

Again there is in both telegrams a gratuitous mention of peace, which has nothing in common with the celebrations of the sailors.

There is not one speech, not one article, in which mention is not made of this, that the aim of all these past orgies is the peace of Europe. At a dinner, which is given by the representatives of the Russian press, everybody speaks of peace. Mr. Zola, who lately wrote about the necessity and even usefulness of war, and Mr. Vogüé, who more than once expressed the same idea, do not say one word about war, but speak only of peace. The meetings of the Chambers are opened with speeches respecting the past celebrations, and the orators affirm that these festivities are the declaration of the peace of Europe.

It is as though a man, coming into some peaceful society, should go out of his way on every occasion to assure the persons present that he has not the slightest intention of knocking out anybody's teeth, smashing eyes, or breaking arms, but means only to pass a peaceable evening. "But nobody has any doubts about that," one feels like saying to him. "But if you have such base intentions, at least do not dare speak of them to us."

In many articles, which were written about these celebrations, there is even a direct and naïve expression of pleasure, because during the festivities no one gave utterance to what by tacit consent it had been decided to conceal from everybody, and what only one incautious man, who was immediately removed by the police, dared to shout, giving expression to the secret thought of all, namely, "A bas l'Allemagne!" Thus children are frequently so happy at having concealed their naughtiness, that their very joy gives them away.

Why should we so rejoice at the fact that no mention was made of war, if we indeed are not thinking of it?

V.

No one is thinking of war, but yet milliards are wasted on military preparations, and, millions of men are under arms in Russia and in France.

"But all this is being done for the security of peace. Si vis pacem, para bellum. L'empire c'est la paix, la republique c'est la paix."

But if it is so, why are the military advantages of our alliance with France in case of a war with Germany explained, not only in all the periodicals and newspapers published for the so-called cultured people, but also in the *Rural Messenger*, a newspaper published by the Russian government for the masses, by means of which these unfortunate masses, deceived by the government, are impressed with this, that "to be friendly with France is also useful and profitable, because, if, beyond all expectation, the above-mentioned powers (Germany, Austria, Italy) should decide to violate the peace with Russia, Russia, though able with God's aid to protect itself and handle a very powerful alliance of adversaries, would not find this to be an easy task, and for a successful struggle great sacrifices and losses would be needed," and so forth (*Rural Messenger*, No. 43, 1893).

And why do they in all the French colleges teach history from a text-book composed by Mr. Lavisse, twenty-first edition, 1889, in which the following passage is found:

"Depuis que l'insurrection de la Commune a été vain-cue, la France n'a plus été troublée. Au lendemain de la guerre, elle s'est remise au travail. Elle a payé aux Alle-mands sans difficulté l'énorme contribution de guerre de cinq milliards. Mais la France a perdu sa renommée mili-taire pendant la guerre de 1870. Elle a perdu une partie de son territoire. Plus de quinze cents mille hommes, qui habitaient nos departements du Haut Rhin, du Bas Rhin et de la Moselle, et qui étaient de bons Français, ont été obligés de devenir Allemands. Ils ne sont pas resignés à leur sort. Ils détestent l'Allemagne; ils espèrent toujours redevenir Français. Mais l'Allemagne tient à sa conquête, et c'est un grand pays, dont tous les habitants aiment sin-cèrement leur patrie et dont les soldats sont braves et dis-ciplinés. Pour reprendre à l'Allemagne ce qu'elle nous a pris, il faut que nous soyons de bons citoyens et de bons soldats. C'est pour que vous deveniez de bons soldats, que vos maîtres vous apprennent l'histoire de la France. L'histoire de la France montre que dans notre pays les fils ont toujours vengé les désastres de leurs pères. Les Français du temps de Charles VII. ont vengé leurs pères vaincus à Crécy, à Poitiers, à Azincourt. C'est à vous, en-fants élèves aujourd'hui dans nos écoles, qu'il appartient de venger vos pères, vaincus à Sédan et à Metz. C'est votre devoir, le grand devoir de votre vie. Vous devez y penser toujours," etc.

At the foot of the page there is a whole series of ques-tions, to correspond to the articles. The questions are as follows: "What did France lose when she lost part of her territory? How many Frenchmen became German with the loss of this territory? Do the French love Germany? What must we do, in order to regain what was taken away from us by Germany?" In addition to these there are also

"*Réflexions sur le Livre VII.*," in which it says that "the children of France must remember our defeats of 1870," that "they must feel on their hearts the burden of this memory," but that "this memory must not discourage them: it should, on the contrary, incite them to bravery."

Thus, if in official speeches peace is mentioned with great persistency, the masses, the younger generations, yes, all the Russians and Frenchmen in general, are imperturbably impressed with the necessity, legality, profitableness, and even virtue of war.

"We are not thinking of war,—we are concerned only about peace."

One feels like asking "Qui, diable, trompe-t-on ici?" if it were necessary to ask this, and if it were not quite clear who the unfortunate cheated are.

The cheated are the same eternally deceived, stupid, labouring masses, the same who with their callous hands have built all these ships, and fortresses, and arsenals, and barracks, and guns, and steamboats, and quays, and moles, and all these palaces, halls, and platforms, and triumphal arches; and have set and printed all these newspapers and books; and have secured and brought all those pheasants, and ortolans, and oysters, and wines, which are consumed by all those men, whom they, again, have nurtured and brought up and sustained,—men who, deceiving the masses, prepare the most terrible calamities for them; the same good-natured, stupid masses, who, displaying their sound, white teeth, have grinned in childish fashion, naïvely enjoying the sight of all the dressed-up admirals and presidents, of the flags fluttering above them, the fireworks, the thundering music, and who will hardly have time to look around, when there shall be no longer any admirals, nor presidents, nor flags, nor music, but there will be only a wet, waste field, hunger, cold, gloom, in front the slaying enemy, behind the goading authorities, blood, wounds, sufferings, rotting corpses, and a senseless, useless death.

And the men like those who now are celebrating at the festivities in Toulon and Paris, will be sitting, after a good dinner, with unfinished glasses of good wine, with a cigar between their teeth, in a dark cloth tent, and will with pins mark down the places on the map where so much food for cannon, composed of the masses, should be left, in order to seize such and such a fortress, and in order to obtain such or such a ribbon or promotion.

VI.

"But there is nothing of the kind, and there are no war-like intentions," we are told. "All there is, is that two nations feeling a mutual sympathy are expressing this sentiment to one another. What harm is there in this, that the representatives of a friendly nation were received with especial solemnity and honour by the representatives of the other nation? What harm is there in it, even if it be admitted that the alliance may have the significance of a protection against a dangerous neighbour, threatening the peace of Europe?"

The harm is this, that all this is a most palpable and bold lie, an unjustifiable, bad lie. The sudden outburst of an exclusive love of the Russians for the French, and of the French for the Russians, is a lie; and our hatred for the Germans, our distrust of them, which is understood by it, is also a lie. And the statement that the aim of all these indecent and mad orgies is the guarantee of European peace, is a still greater lie.

We all know that we have experienced no particular love for the French, neither before, nor even now, even as we have not experienced any hostile feeling toward the Germans.

We are told that Germany has some intentions against Russia, that the Triple Alliance threatens the peace of Europe and us, and that our alliance with France balances the forces, and so guarantees the peace. But this assertion is so obviously absurd, that it makes one feel ashamed to give it a serious denial. For this to be so, that is, for the alliance to guarantee peace, it is necessary that the forces be mathematically even. If now the excess is on the side of the Franco-Russian alliance, the danger is still the same. It is even greater, because, if there was a danger that William, who stood at the head of the European alliance, would violate the peace, there is a much greater danger that France, which cannot get used to the loss of her provinces, will do so. The Triple Alliance was called a league of peace, but for us it was a league of war. Even so now the Franco-Russian alliance cannot present itself as anything else than what it is,—a league of war.

And then, if peace depends on the balance of the powers, how are the units to be determined, between whom the balance is to be established? Now the English say that the alliance between Russia and France menaces them, and that they must, therefore, form another alliance. And into how many units of alliances must Europe be divided, in order that there be a balance? If so, then every man stronger than another in society is already a danger, and the others must form into alliances, to withstand him.

They ask, "What harm is there in this, that France and Russia have expressed their mutual sympathies for the guarantee of peace?" What is bad is, that it is a lie, and a lie is never spoken with impunity, and does not pass unpunished.

The devil is a slayer of men and the father of lies. And the lies always lead to the slaying of men,—in this case more obviously than ever.

In just the same manner as now, the Turkish war was preceded by a sudden outburst of love of our Russians for their brothers, the Slavs, whom no one had known for hundreds of years, while the Germans, the French, the

English have always been incomparably nearer and more closely related to us than Montenegrins, Servians, or Bulgarians. And there began transports, receptions, and festivities, which were fanned by such men as Aksákov and Katkóv, who are mentioned now in Paris as models of patriotism. Then, as now, they spoke of nothing but the mutual sudden outburst of love between the Russians and the Slavs. In the beginning they ate and drank in Moscow, even as now in Paris, and talked nonsense to one another, becoming affected by their own exalted sentiments, spoke of union and peace, and did not say anything about the chief thing, the intentions against Turkey. The newspapers fanned the excitement, and the government by degrees entered into the game. Servia revolted. There began an exchange of diplomatic notes and the publication of semiofficial articles; the newspapers lied more and more, invented and waxed wroth, and the end of it all was that Alexander II., who really did not want any war, could not help but agree to it, and we all know what happened: the destruction of hundreds of thousands of innocent people and the bestialization and dulling of millions.

What was done in Toulon and in Paris, and now continues to be done in the newspapers, obviously leads to the same, or to a still more terrible calamity. Just so all kinds of generals and ministers will at first, to the sounds of "God save the Tsar" and the Marseillaise drink the health of France, of Russia, of the various regiments of the army and the navy; the newspapers will print their lies; the idle crowd of the rich, who do not know what to do with their powers and with their time, will babble patriotic speeches, fanning hatred against Germany, and no matter how peaceful Alexander III. may be, the conditions will be such that he will be unable to decline a war which will be demanded by all those who surround him, by all the newspapers, and, as always seems, by the public opinion of the whole nation. And before we shall have had time to look around, there will appear in the columns of the newspapers the usual, ominous, stupid proclamation:

"By God's grace, we, the most autocratic great Emperor of all Russia, the King of Poland, the Grand Duke of Finland, etc., etc., inform all our faithful subjects that for the good of these dear subjects, entrusted to us by God, we have considered it our duty before God to send them out to slaughter. God be with them," and so forth.

The bells will be rung, and long-haired men will throw gold-embroidered bags over themselves and will begin to pray for the slaughter. And there will begin again the old, well-known, terrible deed. The newspaper writers, who under the guise of patriotism stir people up to hatred and murder, will be about, in the hope of double earnings. Manufacturers, merchants, purveyors of military supplies, will bestir themselves joyfully, expecting double profits. All kinds of officials will bestir themselves, foreseeing a chance to steal more than they usually do. The military authorities will bestir themselves, for they will receive double salaries and rations, and will hope to get for the killing of people all kinds of trifles, which they value very much,—ribbons, crosses, galloons, stars. Idle gentlemen and ladies will bestir themselves, inscribing themselves in advance in the Red Cross, preparing themselves to dress the wounds of those whom their own husbands and brothers will kill, and imagining that they are thus doing a most Christian work.

And, drowning in their hearts their despair by means of songs, debauches, and vódka, hundreds of thousands of simple, good people, torn away from peaceful labour, from their wives, mothers, children, will march, with weapons of murder in their hands, whither they will be driven. They will go to freeze, to starve, to be sick, to die from diseases, and finally they will arrive at the place where they will be killed by the thousand, and they will kill by the thousand, themselves not knowing why, men whom they have never seen and who have done them and can do them no harm.

And when there shall be collected so many sick, wounded, and killed that nobody will have the time to pick them up, and when the air shall already be so infected by this rotting food for cannon that even the authorities will feel uncomfortable, then they will stop for awhile, will somehow manage to pick up the wounded, will haul off and somewhere throw into a pile the sick, and will bury the dead, covering them with lime, and again they will lead on the whole crowd of the deceived, and will continue to lead them on in this manner until those who have started the whole thing will get tired of it, or until those who needed it will get what they needed.

And again will men become infuriated, brutalized, and bestialized, and love will be diminished in the world, and the incipient Christianization of humanity will be delayed for decades and for centuries. And again will the people, who gain thereby, begin to say with assurance that, if there is a war, this means that it is necessary, and again they will begin to prepare for it the future generations, by corrupting them from childhood.

VII.

And so, when there appear such patriotic manifestations as were the Toulon celebrations, which, though still
at a distance, in advance bind the wills of men and oblige
them to commit those customary malefactions which always result from patriotism, every one who understands
the significance of these celebrations cannot help but
protest against everything which is tacitly included in
them. And so, when the journalists say in print that all the
Russians sympathize with what took place at Kronstadt,
Toulon, and Paris; that this alliance for life and death is
confirmed by the will of the whole nation; and when the
Russian minister of education assures the French ministers that his whole company, the Russian children, the
learned, and the authors, share his sentiments; or when
the commander of the Russian squadron assures the
French that the whole of Russia will be grateful to them
for their reception; and when the chief priests speak for
their flocks and assure the French that their prayers for
the life of the most august house have reëchoed joyfully
in the hearts of the Russian *Tsar-loving* nation; and when
the Russian ambassador in Paris, who is considered to
be the representative of the Russian nation, says after a
dinner of ortolans à la soubise et logopédes glacés, with
a glass of champagne *Grand Moët* in his hand, that all
Russian hearts are beating in unison with his heart, which
is filled with a sudden outburst of exclusive love for fair
France (la belle France),—we, the people who are free

from the stultification, consider it our sacred duty, not only for our own sakes, but also for the sake of tens of millions of Russians, in the most emphatic manner to protest against it and to declare that our hearts do not beat in unison with the hearts of the journalists, ministers of education, commanders of squadrons, chief priests, and ambassadors, but, on the contrary, are full to the brim with indignation and loathing for that harmful lie and that evil which they consciously and unconsciously disseminate with their acts and their speeches. Let them drink *Moët* as much as they please, and let them write articles and deliver addresses in their own name, but we, all the Christians, who recognize ourselves as such, cannot admit that we are bound by everything that these men say and write. We cannot admit it, because we know what is concealed beneath all these drunken transports, speeches, and embraces, which do not resemble the confirmation of peace, as we are assured, but rather those orgies and that drunkenness to which evil-doers abandon themselves when they prepare themselves for a joint crime.

VIII.

About four years ago,—the first swallow of the Toulon spring,—a certain French agitator in favour of a war with Germany came to Russia for the purpose of preparing the Franco-Russian alliance, and he visited us in the country. He arrived at our house when we were working in the mowing. At breakfast, as we returned home, we made the acquaintance of the guest, and he immediately proceeded to tell us how he had fought, had been in captivity, had run away from it, and how he had made a patriotic vow, of which he was apparently proud, that he would not stop agitating a war against Germany until the integrity and glory of France should be reëstablished.

In our circle all the convictions of our guest as to how necessary an alliance between Russia and France was for the reëstablishment of the former borders of France and its might and glory, and for making us secure against the malevolent intentions of Germany, were of no avail to him. In reply to his arguments that France could not be at peace so long as the provinces taken from it were not returned to it, we said that similarly Prussia could not be at rest, so long as it had not paid back for Jena, and that, if the French "revanche" should now be successful, the Germans would have to pay them back, and so on without end.

In reply to his arguments that the French were obliged to save their brothers, who had been torn away from them, we said that the condition of the inhabitants, of the majority of the inhabitants, of the working people in Alsace-Lorraine, was hardly any worse under German rule than it had been under France, and that, because some Alsatians preferred to belong to France rather than to Germany, and he, our guest, found it desirable to reestablish the glory of French arms, it was not worth while, either to begin those terrible calamities which result from war, or even to sacrifice one single human life.

In reply to his arguments that it was all very well for us to speak thus, since we had not experienced the same, and that we should be speaking differently, if we had the Baltic provinces and Poland taken away from us, we said that even from the political standpoint the loss of Poland and of the Baltic provinces could not be a calamity for us, but might rather be considered an advantage, since it would diminish the necessity for a military force and the expenses of state; and from the Christian point of view we never could permit a war, since a war demanded the killing of men, whereas Christianity not only forbade every murder, but even demanded that we do good to all men, considering all, without distinction of nationalities, as our brothers. The Christian state, we said, which enters upon war, to be consistent, must not only haul down the crosses from the churches, turn all the churches into buildings for different purposes, give the clergy other offices, and, above all, prohibit the Gospel, but must also renounce all the demands of morality which result from the Christian law. "C'est à prendre ou à laisser," we said. But until Christianity was abolished, it would be possible to entice men to war only by cunning and deceit, as indeed is being done nowadays. We see this cunning and deception, and so cannot submit to it. As there was no music, no champagne, nothing intoxicating about us, our guest only shrugged his shoulders and with customary French amiability remarked that he was very thankful for the fine reception accorded to him in our house, but that he was sorry that his ideas were not treated in the same way.

IX.

After this conversation we went to the mowing, and there he, in the hope of finding more sympathy for his ideas among the masses, asked me to translate to the peasant Prokófi, an old, sickly man, with an enormous rupture, who none the less stuck to his work, and was my companion in the mowing, his plan of attacking the Germans, which was to squeeze the Germans, who were between the French and the Russians, from both sides. The Frenchman gave an ocular demonstration of this to Prokófi, by touching from two sides Prokófi's sweaty hempen shirt with his white fingers. I recall Prokófi's good-naturedly scornful surprise, when I explained to him the Frenchman's words and gestures. The proposition to squeeze the Germans from both sides was apparently taken by Prokófi as a joke, for he would not admit the idea that a grown man and a scholar should calmly and when he was sober talk of the desirability of war.

"Well, if we squeeze the German from both sides," he replied jestingly to what he thought was a joke, "he will have no place to go to. We must give him room."

I translated this to my guest.

"Dites lui que nous aimons les Russes," he said.

These words obviously startled Prokófi even more than the proposition to squeeze the German, and provoked a certain sentiment of suspicion.

"Who is he?" Prokófi asked me, with mistrust, indicating my guest with his head.

I told him that he was a Frenchman, a rich man.

"What is his business?" Prokófi asked me.

When I explained to him that he had come to invite the Russians to form an alliance with France in case of a war with Germany, Prokófi apparently became quite dissatisfied, and, turning to the women, who were sitting near a haycock, he shouted at them in a strong voice, which involuntarily betrayed the feelings which this conversation had provoked in him, that they should go and rake up the unraked hay.

"Come now, you crows! Have you fallen asleep? Come! Much time we have to squeeze the German! We have not finished the mowing yet, and it looks likely that we shall be mowing on Wednesday," he said. And then, as though fearing to offend the stranger by such a remark, he added, displaying his half-worn-off teeth in a good-natured smile, "You had better come and work with us, and send the German, too. When we get through working, we shall have a good time. Well take the German along. They are just such folk as we." And, having said this, Prokófi took his muscular arm out of the crotch of the fork, on which he had been leaning, threw the fork over his shoulders, and went away to the women.

"Oh, le brave homme!" the polite Frenchman exclaimed, smiling. And with this he then concluded his diplomatic mission to the Russian people.

The sight of these so radically different men,—the one beaming with freshness, alacrity, elegance, the well-fed Frenchman, in a silk hat and long overcoat of the latest fashion, energetically illustrating with his white hands, unused to labour, how to squeeze the Germans, and the sight of the dishevelled Prokófi, with hay-seed in his hair, dried up from work, sunburnt, always tired and always working, in spite of his immense rupture, with fingers swollen from work, with his loosely hanging homespun trousers, battered bast shoes, jogging along with an immense forkful of hay over his shoulder in that indolent pace of a labouring man, which economizes motion,—the sight of these two so radically different men elucidated to me then many things, and has occurred to me now, after the Toulon-Paris celebrations. One of them personified all those men, nurtured by the labours of the masses, who later use these masses as food for cannon; and Prokófi personified to me that food for cannon, which nurtures and makes secure the men who dispose of it.

X.

"But France has been deprived of two provinces,—two children have been violently removed from their mother. But Russia cannot permit Germany to prescribe laws to it and to deprive it of its historic destiny in the East,—it cannot tolerate the chance of having its provinces, the Baltic provinces, Poland, the Caucasus, taken from it, as was done in the case of France. But Germany cannot tolerate the possibility of losing its prerogatives, which it has gained through so many sacrifices. But England cannot yield its supremacy on the seas to any one." And, having spoken such words, it is generally assumed that a Frenchman, a Russian, a German, an Englishman must be prepared to sacrifice everything in order to regain the lost provinces, to establish their predominance in the East, to maintain their unity and power, their supremacy on the seas, and so forth.

It is assumed that the sentiment of patriotism is, in the first place, a sentiment which is always inherent in men, and, in the second, such an exalted moral sentiment that, if it is absent, it has to be evoked in those who do not have it. But neither is correct. I have passed half a century among the Russian masses, and among the great majority of the real Russian people I have in all that time never seen or heard even once any manifestation or expression of this sentiment of patriotism, if we do not count those patriotic phrases, which are learned by rote during military service or are repeated from books by the most frivolous and spoiled men of the nation. I have never heard any expression of patriotic sentiments from the people; but, I have, on the contrary, frequently heard the most serious and respectable men from among the masses giving utterance to the most absolute indifference and even contempt for all kinds of manifestations of patriotism. The same thing I have observed among the labouring classes of other nations, and I have often been assured of the same by cultured Frenchmen, Germans, and Englishmen concerning their own working people.

The working people are too busy with the all-absorbing business of supporting themselves and their families, to be interested in those political questions, which present themselves as the chief motive of patriotism,—the questions of Russia's influence in the East, the unity of Germany, or the restitution of the lost provinces to France, or the acts of this or that part of one state toward another, and so forth, do not interest them, not only because they hardly ever know the conditions under which these questions have arisen, but also because the interests of their lives are quite independent of the political interests. It is always very much a matter of indifference to a man from the masses, where certain borders will be marked down, or to whom Constantinople will belong, or whether Saxony or Brunswick will be a member of the German union, or whether Australia or Matabeleland will belong to England, or even to what government he will have to pay taxes and to what army he will have to send his sons; but it is always very important for him to know how much he will have to pay in taxes, how long he has to serve, and how much he will receive for his labour,—and these are questions that are quite independent of the common political interests. It is for this reason that, in spite of all the intensified means used by the governments for the inoculation of the masses with a patriotism which is alien to them and for the suppression of the ideas of socialism, which are developing among them, the socialism more and more penetrates into the masses, and the patriotism, which is so carefully inoculated by the governments, is not only not adopted by the masses, but is disappearing more and more, maintaining itself only among the upper classes, to whom it is advantageous. If it happens that at times patriotism takes hold of the popular crowd, as was the case in Paris, this is only so when the masses are subjected to an intensified hypnotic influence by the governments and the ruling classes, and the patriotism is maintained among the masses only so long at this influence lasts.

Thus, for example, in Russia, where patriotism, in the form of love and loyalty for the faith, the Tsar, and the country, is inoculated in the masses with extraordinary tension and with the use of all the tools at the command of the governments, such as the church, the school, the press, and all kinds of solemnities, the Russian labouring classes,—one hundred millions of the Russian nation,—in spite of Russia's unearned reputation as a nation that is particularly devoted to its faith, its Tsar, and its country, are most free from the deception of patriotism and from loyalty to faith, the Tsar, and country. The men of the masses for the most part do not know their Orthodox, state faith, to which they are supposed to be so loyal, and when they come to know it, they immediately give it up and become rationalists, that is, accept a faith which it is impossible to attack or to defend; on their Tsar they, in spite of the constant and persistent influences brought to bear upon them, look as upon all the powers of violence, if not with condemnation, at least with absolute indifference; but their country, if by that we do not mean their village or township, they do not know at all, or, if they do, they do not distinguish it from any other countries, so that, as Russian colonists used to go to Austria and to Turkey, they now with just as much indifference settle in Russia, outside of Russia, in Turkey or in China.

XI.

My old friend D——, who in the winter lived alone in the country, while his wife, whom he went to see but rarely, lived in Paris, used to talk during the long autumn evenings with an illiterate, but very clever and respectable peasant, an elder, who came in the evening to report, and my friend told him, among other things, of the superiority of the French political order over our own. This was on the eve of the last Polish insurrection and the interference of the French government in our affairs. The patriotic Russian newspapers at that time burned with indignation on account of such interference, and so heated up the ruling classes that they talked of a war with France.

My friend, who had read the papers, told the elder also of these relations between Russia and France. Submitting to the tone of the papers, my friend said that if there should be any war (he was an old soldier), he would serve and fight against France. At that time the "revanche" against the French seemed necessary to the Russians on account of Sevastopol.

"But why should we wage war?" asked the elder.

"How can we permit France to manage our affairs?"

"But you say yourself that things are better arranged with them than with us," the elder said, quite seriously. "Let them arrange matters in our country, too."

My friend told me that this reflection so startled him that he was absolutely at a loss what to say, and only laughed, as laugh those who awaken from a deceptive dream.

Such reflections one may hear from any sober Russian labouring man, if only he is not under any hypnotic influence of the government. They talk of the love of the Russian masses for their faith, their Tsar, and their government, and yet there will not be found one commune of peasants in the whole of Russia, which would hesitate for a moment, which of the two places to choose for its colonization,—Russia, with the Tsar, the little father, as they write in books, and with the holy Orthodox faith in its adored country, but with less and worse land, or without the little father, the white Tsar, and without the Orthodox faith, somewhere outside of Russia, in Prussia, China, Turkey, Austria, but with some greater and better advantages, as indeed we have seen before and see at present. For every Russian peasant the question as to what government he will be under (since he knows that, no matter under what government he may be, he will be fleeced just the same) has incomparably less meaning than the question as to whether, I will not say the water is good, but as to whether the clay is soft and as to whether there will be a good crop of cabbage.

But it may be thought that the indifference of the Russians is due to this, that any other government under whose power they may come will certainly be better than the Russian, because in Europe there is not one that is worse than the Russian; but that is not so: so far as I know, we have seen the same in the case of the English, Dutch, German immigrants in America, and of all the other colonists in Russia.

The transference of the European nations from the power of one government to another, from the Turkish to the Austrian, or from the French to the German, changes the condition of the nations so little that in no case can they provoke the dissatisfaction of the working classes, so long as they are not artificially subjected to the suggestions of the governments and the ruling classes.

XII.

People generally adduce, in proof of the existence of patriotism, the manifestations of patriotic sentiments in a nation during a time of all kinds of celebrations, as, for example, in Russia during a coronation or the meeting of the emperor after the calamity of the seventeenth of October, or in France during the proclamation of war against Prussia, or in Germany during the festivities of victory, or during the Franco-Russian celebrations.

But it ought to be known how these manifestations are prepared. In Russia, for example, people are especially dressed up by the village commune and the owners of factories to meet and welcome the emperor whenever he passes through a given locality.

The transports of the masses are generally prepared artificially by those who need them, and the degree of transport expressed by the crowd shows only the degree of the art of the arrangers of these transports. This business has long been practised, and so the specialists in arranging such transports have reached a high degree of virtuosity in these arrangements. When Alexander II. was still an heir apparent, and was in command, as is usually the case, of the Preobrázhenski regiment, he once drove out after dinner to the regiment in camp. The moment his carriage appeared, the soldiers, coatless as they were, rushed out to meet him, and with such transport welcomed, as they say, their most august commander, that all ran a race behind his carriage, and many of them made the sign of the cross while on a run, looking all the time at the heir apparent. All those who saw this meeting were deeply touched by this naïve loyalty and love of the Russian soldiers for their Tsar and his heir, and by that sincere religious and apparently unprepared transport which was expressed in the faces, the motions, and especially in the signs of the cross, which the soldiers made. However, all that was done artificially and prepared in the following manner: after the inspection of the previous day the heir said to the brigade commander that he would drive up the next day to the regiment.

"When are we to expect your Imperial Majesty?"

"In all probability in the evening. Only, please, no preparations."

The moment the heir drove off, the brigade commander called together the commanders of the companies and gave the order that on the following day all the soldiers were to appear in clean shirts, and, as soon as they saw the heir's carriage, which the signallers were to announce, they were to run at haphazard after the carriage, shouting "Hurrah!" and that, at the same time, every tenth man in the company was to run and make the sign of the cross. The sergeants drew up the companies, and, counting the soldiers, stopped at every tenth man: "One, two, three ... eight, nine, ten,—Sidorénko—the sign of the cross; one, two, three, four ... Ivánov—the sign of the cross...." Everything was carried out as by command, and the impression of transport was complete, both on the heir apparent and on all the persons present, even on the soldiers and the officers, and even on the commander of the brigade, who had invented all that. Just so, though less coarsely, they do in all places, wherever there are any patriotic manifestations. Thus the Franco-Russian celebrations, which present themselves to us as free expressions of the people's sentiments, did not originate with the people, but were, on the contrary, very artfully and quite obviously prepared and provoked by the French government.

"The moment the arrival of the Russian sailors became known," I am again quoting the same *Rural Messenger*, the official organ, which collects its information from all the other newspapers, "committees for the arrangement of celebrations were being formed, not only in all the large and small cities lying on the route from Toulon to Paris, a considerable distance, but also in a large number of towns and villages which lie quite to either side of this route. Everywhere a subscription was opened for contributions to meet the expenses for these celebrations. Many cities sent deputations to Paris to our imperial ambassador, imploring him to let the sailors visit their cities even for one day or even for one hour. The municipal governments of all those cities in which our sailors were ordered to stay set aside vast sums, averaging more than one hundred thousand roubles, for the arrangement of all kinds of festivities and amusements, and expressed their willingness to expend even greater sums, as much as should be needed, provided the welcome and the celebrations should be as magnificent as possible.

"In Paris itself a private committee collected, in addition to the sum set aside by the city government for this purpose, an immense sum by private subscription, also for the arrangement of amusements, and the French government assigned more than one hundred thousand roubles for expenses incurred by the ministers and other authorities in welcoming the guests. In many cities, where our sailors will not set foot at all, they none the less decided to celebrate the first of October with all kinds of festivities in honour of Russia. A vast number of cities and provinces decided to send special deputations to Toulon and Paris, in order to welcome the Russian guests and to offer them presents to remember France by, or to send to them addresses and telegrams of welcome. It was decided everywhere to consider the first of October a national holiday and to dismiss the pupils of all the educational institutions for that day, and in Paris for two days. Officials of lower rank had their penalties remitted, that they might gratefully remember the joyful day for France,—the first of October.

"To make it easier for those who wished to visit Toulon and take part in the welcome to the Russian squadron, the railways lowered the rates to one-half and sent out special trains."

And thus, when by means of a whole series of universal, simultaneous measures, which the government can always take by dint of the power which it has in its hands, a certain part of the nation, preëminently the scum of the people, the city crowd, is brought to a condition of abnormal excitement, they say: "Behold, this is the free expression of the will of the whole nation." Manifestations like those which just took place in Toulon and in Paris, which in Germany take place at the meeting of the emperor or of Bismarck, or at manœuvres in Lorraine, and which are constantly repeated in Russia at every meeting circumstanced with solemnity, prove only this, that the means of an artificial excitation of the people, which now are in the hands of the governments and the ruling classes, are so powerful that the governments and the ruling classes, which are in possession of them, are always able at will to provoke any kind of a patriotic manifestation they may wish by rousing the patriotic sentiments of the masses.

Nothing, on the contrary, proves the absence of patriotism in the masses with such obviousness as those tense efforts which now are made by the governments and the ruling classes for the artificial excitation of patriotism, and the insignificant results which are obtained in spite of all the efforts.

If patriotic sentiments are so proper to the nations, they should be permitted to manifest themselves freely, and should not be provoked by all kinds of exclusive and artificial means, applied on every possible occasion. Let them even for a time, for one year, stop in Russia compelling all the people, as they are doing now, upon the accession of every Tsar, to swear allegiance to him; let them at every divine service stop solemnly repeating several times the customary prayers for the Tsar; let them stop celebrating his birthdays and name-days with ringing of bells, illumination, and the prohibition to work; let them stop everywhere hanging out and displaying representations of him; let them stop, in prayer-books, almanacs, text-books, printing his name and the names of his family, and even the pronouns referring to him, in capitals; let them stop glorifying him in special books and newspapers printed for the purpose; let them stop imprisoning men for the slightest disrespectful word uttered concerning the Tsar,—let them stop doing all that for a time only, and then we should see how proper it is for the masses, for the real labouring masses, for Prokófi, for elder Iván, and for all the men of the Russian masses,—as the nation is made to believe and as all the foreigners are convinced of it,—to worship the Tsar, who in one way or another turns them over into the hands of a landed proprietor or of the rich in general. So it is in Russia; but let them similarly stop in Germany, France, Italy, England,

America doing all that which is done there with the same tension by the ruling classes in order to rouse patriotism and loyalty and submission to the existing government, and we should see in how far this imaginary patriotism is characteristic of the nations of our time.

But, as it is, the masses are stultified from childhood by all possible means, by school-books, divine services, sermons, books, newspapers, verses, monuments, which all tend in one and the same direction; then they select by force or bribery a few thousands of the people, and when these assembled thousands, joined by all the loafers who are always happy to be present at any spectacle, to the sounds of cannon-shots and of music, and at the sight of every kind of splendour and light begin to shout what the leaders shout to them, we are told that this is an expression of the sentiments of the whole nation. But, in the first place, these thousands, or, if it is a great crowd, these tens of thousands, who shout something at such celebrations, form but a tiny, a ten-thousandth part of the whole nation; in the second place, out of these tens of thousands of shouting men, who wave their hats, the greater part are either collected by force, as is the case with us in Russia, or artificially provoked by some enticement; in the third place, among all these thousands, there are scarcely tens who know what it is all about, and all the rest would as gladly shout and wave their hats if the very opposite took place; and, in the fourth place, the police are always present, and they will make any one shut up if he does not shout what the government wants and demands shall be shouted, and lock him up at once, as was done with much force during the Franco-Russian festivities.

In France they welcomed with equal enthusiasm the war with Russia under Napoleon I., and then Alexander

I., against whom the war was waged, and then again Napoleon, and again the allies, and Bourbon, and Orleans, and the Republic, and Napoleon III., and Boulanger; and in Russia they acclaim with the same enthusiasm, to-day Peter, to-morrow Catherine, the next day Paul, Alexander, Constantine, Nicholas, the Duke of Leuchtenberg, the brother Slavs, the King of Prussia, the French sailors, and all those whom the government wants them to welcome. The same happens in England, America, Germany, Italy.

What in our time is called patriotism is, on the one hand, only a certain mood, which is constantly produced and maintained in the masses by the schools, the religion, the venal press, having such a tendency as the government demands, and, on the other, a temporary excitation, produced with exclusive means by the ruling classes, in the masses, who stand on a lower moral and even mental plane,—an excitation, which later is given out as a constant expression of the will of the whole nation. The patriotism of the oppressed nationalities does not form an exception to this. It is as little characteristic of the working classes, and is artificially inculcated upon them by the upper classes.

XIII.

"But if the men of the masses do not experience the sentiment of patriotism, this is due to the fact that they have not yet reached that exalted sentiment, which is characteristic of every cultured man. If they do not experience this exalted sentiment, it has to be educated in them. It is this that the government is doing."

Thus generally speak the men of the ruling classes, with such full confidence that patriotism is an exalted sentiment, that the naïve men of the masses, who do not experience it, consider themselves at fault, because they do not experience this sentiment, and try to assure themselves that they experience it, or at least pretend that they do.

But what is this exalted sentiment, which, in the opinion of the ruling classes, ought to be educated in the nations?

This sentiment is in its most precise definition nothing but a preference shown to one's own state or nation in comparison with any other state or nation, a sentiment which is fully expressed in the German patriotic song, "Deutschland, Deutschland über alles," in which we need only substitute *Russland, Frankreich, Italien,* or any other state for *Deutschland,* and we shall get the clearest formula of the exalted sentiment of patriotism. It may be that this sentiment is very desirable and useful for the governments and the integrity of the state, but one cannot help but observe that this sentiment is not at all exalted, but, on the contrary, very stupid and very immoral: stupid, because, if every state will consider itself better than any other, it is obvious that they will all be in the wrong; and immoral, because it inevitably leads every man who experiences the feeling to try to obtain advantages for his own state and nation, at the expense of other states and nations—a tendency which is directly opposed to the fundamental moral law recognized by all men: not to do unto another what we do not wish to have done to ourselves.

Patriotism may have been a virtue in the ancient world, when it demanded of man that he serve the highest ideal accessible to him at the time,—the ideal of his country. But how can patriotism be a virtue in our time, when it demands of men what is directly opposed to what forms the ideal of our religion and morality,—not the recognition of the equality and brotherhood of all men, but the recognition of one state and nationality as predominating over all the others. This sentiment is in our time not only not a virtue, but unquestionably a vice; no such sentiment of patriotism in its true sense does or can exist in our time, because the material and moral foundations for it are lacking.

Patriotism could have some sense in the ancient world, when every nation, more or less homogeneous in its structure, professing one and the same state religion, and submitting to the same unlimited power of its supreme, deified ruler, appeared to itself as an island in the ocean of the barbarians, which ever threatened to inundate it.

We can see how with such a state of affairs, patriotism, that is, the desire to ward off the attacks of the barbarians, who were not only prepared to destroy the social order, but who also threatened wholesale plundering and murder, with the enslavement of men and the rape of women, was a natural feeling, and we can see why a man, to free himself and his compatriots from such calamities, could have preferred his nation to all the others, and could experience a hostile feeling toward the barbarians around him, and could kill them, in order to protect his nation.

But what significance can this sentiment have in our Christian time? On what ground and for what purpose can a man of our time, a Russian, go and kill Frenchmen or Germans, or a Frenchman Germans, when he knows full well, no matter how little educated he may be, that the men of the other state and nation, against which they are rousing his patriotic hostility, are not barbarians, but just such Christians as he, frequently of the same faith and profession with him, desiring like him nothing but peace and a peaceful exchange of labour, and that, besides, they are for the most part united with him either by the interests of common labour, or by commercial or spiritual interests, or by all together? Thus frequently the men of another country are nearer and more indispensable to a man than his own countrymen, as is the case with labourers who are connected with employers of other nationalities, and as is the case with commercial people, and especially with scholars and artists.

Besides, the conditions of life themselves have so changed now that what we call our country, what we are supposed to distinguish from everything else, has ceased to be something clearly defined, as it was with the ancients, where the men forming one country belonged to one nationality, one state, and one faith. We can understand the patriotism of an Egyptian, a Jew, a Greek, who, defending his country, was at the same time defending his faith, and his nationality, and his home, and his state.

But in what way will in our time be expressed the patriotism of an Irishman in the United States, who by his faith belongs to Rome, by his nationality to Ireland, by his state allegiance to the United States? In the same condition are a Bohemian in Austria, a Pole in Russia, Prussia, and Austria, a Hindoo in England, a Tartar and an Armenian in Russia and in Turkey. But, even leaving out these men of the separate conquered nationalities, the men of the most homogeneous states, such as are Russia, France, Prussia, can no longer experience that sentiment of patriotism, which was peculiar to the ancients, because frequently all the chief interests of their life (sometimes their domestic ones,—they are married to women of another nation; the economic ones,—their capital is abroad; their spiritual, scientific, or artistic ones) are not in their own country, but outside it, in that state against which the government is rousing his patriotic hatred.

But most of all is patriotism impossible in our time, because, no matter how much we have tried for eighteen hundred years to conceal the meaning of Christianity, it has none the less trickled through into our life, and is guiding it in such a way that the coarsest and most stupid of men cannot help but see the absolute incompatibility of patriotism with those moral rules by which they live.

XIV.

Patriotism was necessary for the formation, out of heterogeneous nationalities, of strong, united kingdoms, protected against the barbarians. But as soon as the Christian enlightenment transformed all these kingdoms alike from within, by giving them the same foundations, patriotism not only became unnecessary, but was also the one barrier against that union of the nations for which they are prepared by dint of their Christian consciousness.

Patriotism is in our time the cruel tradition of a long-gone-by period of time, which holds itself only through inertia and because the governments and the ruling classes feel that with this patriotism is connected not only their power, but also their existence, and so with care and cunning and violence rouse and sustain it in the nations. Patriotism is in our time like the scaffolding, which at one time was necessary for the construction of the walls of a building, but which now, though it only interferes with the proper use of the building, is not taken down, because its existence is advantageous for some persons.

Among the Christian nations there has for a long time ceased to exist any cause for discord, and there can be no such cause. It is even impossible to imagine why and how Russian and German labourers, who peacefully work together near the border and in the capital cities, should begin to quarrel among themselves. And much less can we imagine any hostility between, let us say, a Kazán peasant, who supplies a German with corn, and the German, who supplies him with scythes and machines, and similarly among French, German, and Italian labourers. It is even ridiculous to talk of quarrels among the scholars, artists, writers of various nationalities, who live by the same interests, that are independent of nationality and the state structure.

But the governments cannot leave the nations alone, that is, in peaceful relations among themselves, because the chief, if not the only justification of the existence of the governments consists in making peace between the nations, that is, in allaying their hostile relations. And so the governments provoke these hostile relations under the guise of patriotism, and then make it appear that they are making peace among the nations. It is something like what a gipsy does, who pours some pepper under his horse's tail, and lashes it in the stall, and then leads it out, while hanging on to the bridle, pretending that he has the hardest time to restrain the mettled horse.

We are assured that the governments are concerned about preserving the peace among the nations. In what way do they preserve this peace?

People are living along the Rhine in peaceful intercourse among themselves,—suddenly, in consequence of all kinds of disputes and intrigues between the kings and emperors, war breaks out, and the French government finds it necessary to recognize some of these inhabitants as Frenchmen. Ages pass, men have become accustomed to this state of affairs; again there begin hostilities between the governments of the great nations, and war breaks out on the slightest pretence, and the Germans find it necessary to recognize these inhabitants once more as Germans, and in all the French and the Germans ill-will flames up toward one another. Or Germans and Russians are living peacefully near the border, peacefully exchanging their labour and the products of labour, and suddenly the same institutions which exist only in the name of the pacification of the nations begin to quarrel, to do one foolish thing after another, and are not able to invent anything better than the coarsest childish method of self-inflicted punishment, if only they can thus have their will and do something nasty to their adversary (which in this case is especially advantageous, since not those who start a customs war, but others, suffer from it); thus the Customs War between Russia and Germany was lately started. Then, with the aid of the newspapers, there flames up a malevolent feeling, which is still farther fanned by the Franco-Russian celebrations, and which, before we know it, may lead to a sanguinary war.

I have cited the last two examples of the manner in which the governments affect the people by rousing in them a hostile feeling toward other nations, because they are contemporary; but there is not one war in all history, which was not provoked by the governments, by the governments alone, independently of the advantages to the nations, to which war, even if it is successful, is always harmful.

The governments assure the nations that they are in danger of an incursion from other nations and from internal enemies, and that the only salvation from this danger consists in the slavish obedience of the nations to their governments. This is most obvious in the time of revolutions and dictatorships, and this takes place at all times and in all places, wherever there is power. Every government explains its existence and justifies all its violence by insisting that, if it did not exist, things would be worse. By assuring the nations that they are in danger, the governments subject them to themselves. When the nations submit to the governments, these governments compel these nations to attack the other nations. In this manner the nations find confirmed the assurances of their governments in regard to the danger from being attacked by other nations.

Divide et impera.

Patriotism in its simplest, clearest, and most unquestionable significance is for the rulers nothing but a tool for attaining their ambitious and selfish ends, and for the ruled a renunciation of human dignity, reason, conscience, and a slavish submission to those who are in power. Thus is patriotism actually preached, wherever it is preached.

Patriotism is slavery.

The advocates of peace through arbitration judge like this: two animals cannot divide their prey otherwise than by fighting, as do children, barbarians, and barbarous nations. But sensible people settle their differences by discussion, conviction, the transmission of the solution of the question to disinterested, sensible men. Even thus must the sensible nations of our time act. These reflections seem quite correct. The nations of our time have reached an age of discretion, are not hostile to one another, and should be able to settle their differences in a peaceable manner. But the reflection is correct only in reference to the nations, to the nations alone, if they were not under the power of their governments. But the nations which submit to their governments cannot be sensible, because submission to the governments is already a sign of the greatest senselessness.

How can we talk of the sensibleness of men who promise in advance to do everything (including the murder of men) which the government, that is, certain men who have accidentally come to hold this position, may command them to do?

Men who are able to accept such a duty of unflinching submission to what certain strangers will, from St. Petersburg, Vienna, Paris, command them to do, cannot be sensible, and the governments, that is, the men who possess such power, can still less be sensible, and cannot help abusing it,—they cannot help losing their minds from such a senselessly terrible power. For that reason the peace among the nations cannot be attained by any sensible means, through conventions, through arbitrations, so long as there exists a submission to the governments, which is always senseless and always pernicious.

But the submission of men to the governments will always exist, so long as there is any patriotism, because every power is based on patriotism, that is, on the readiness of men, for the sake of defending their nation, their country, that is, the state, against supposed dangers that are threatening it, to submit to the power.

On this patriotism was based the power of the French kings over the whole nation previous to the Revolution; on the same patriotism was based the power of the Committee of Public Safety after the Revolution; on the same patriotism was reared the power of Napoleon (as consul and as emperor); and on the same patriotism, after the downfall of Napoleon, was established the power of the Bourbons, and later of the Republic, and of Louis Philippe, and again of the Republic, and again of Bonaparte, and again of the Republic, and on the same patriotism came very near being established the power of Mr. Boulanger.

It is terrible to say so, but there does not exist, and there has not existed, a case of aggregate violence committed by one set of men against another which has not been committed in the name of patriotism. In the name of patriotism the Russians fought with the French, and the French with the Russians, and in the name of patriotism the Russians and the French are now preparing themselves to wage war against the Germans,—to fight from two flanks. But war is not all,—in the name of patriotism the Russians crush the Poles, and the Germans the Slavs; in the name of patriotism the Communists killed the Versaillians, and the Versaillians, the Communists.

XV.

It would seem that with the dissemination of culture, of improved means of locomotion, of frequent intercourse among the men of the various nations, in connection with the diffusion of the press, and, above all, in connection with the complete absence of danger from other nations, the deception of patriotism ought to become harder and harder, and ought in the end to become impossible.

But the point is, that these same means of a universal external culture, of improved methods of locomotion, and of intercommunication, and above all, of the press, which the governments have seized upon and seize upon more and more, give them now such a power of exciting in the nations hostile feelings toward one another, that, though on the one hand the obviousness of the useless-ness and harm of patriotism has increased, there has, on the other, increased the power of the governments and of the ruling classes to influence the masses, by rousing patriotism in them.

The difference between what was and what now is consists only in this, that, since now a much greater number of men share in the advantages which patriotism af-fords to the upper classes, a much greater number of men take part in the dissemination and maintenance of this wonderful superstition.

The more difficult it is to maintain the power, the greater and greater is the number of men with whom the government shares it.

Formerly a small group of rulers had the power,—emperors, kings, dukes, their officials, and warriors; but now the participants in this power and in the advantages which it affords are not only the officials and the clergy, but also capitalists, great and small, the landowners, bankers, members of Chambers, teachers, rural officers, scholars, even artists, and especially journalists. And all these persons consciously and unconsciously spread the deception of patriotism, which is indispensable to them for the maintenance of their advantageous position. And the deception, thanks to the fact that the means of deception have become more powerful and that now an ever-growing number of men are taking part in it, is produced so successfully that, in spite of the great difficulty of deceiving, the degree of the deception remains the same.

One hundred years ago, the illiterate masses, who had no conception as to who composed their government and as to what nations surrounded them, blindly obeyed those local officials and gentry, whose slaves they were. And it sufficed for the government by means of bribes and rewards to keep these officials and this gentry in their power, in order that the masses might obediently do what was demanded of them. But now, when the masses for the most part can read and more or less know of whom their government is composed, and what nations surround them; when the men of the masses constantly move about with ease from one place to another, bringing to the masses information about what is going on in the world, a mere demand to carry out the commands of the government no longer suffices: it becomes necessary to obscure the true conceptions which the masses have concerning life, and to impress them with improper ideas concerning the conditions of their life and concerning the relation of other nations toward them.

And so, thanks to the diffusion of the press, of the rudiments, and of the means of communication, the governments, having their agents everywhere, by means of decrees, church sermons, the schools, the newspapers inculcate on the masses the wildest and most perverse conceptions about their advantages, about the relation of the peoples among themselves, about their properties and intentions; and the masses, which are so crushed by labour that they have no time and no chance to understand the significance and verify the correctness of those conceptions which are inculcated upon them, and of those demands which are made on them in the name of their good, submit to them without a murmur.

But the men from the masses who free themselves from constant labour and who educate themselves, and who, it would seem, should be able to understand the deception which is practised upon them, are subjected to such an intensified effect of menaces, bribery, and hypnotization by the governments, that they almost without an exception pass over to the side of the governments and, accepting advantageous and well-paid positions as teachers, priests, officers, officials, become participants in the dissemination of the deception which ruins their fellow men. It is as though at the door of education stood a snare, into which inevitably fall those who in one way or another leave the masses that are absorbed in labour.

At first, as one comes to understand the cruelty of the deception, there involuntarily rises an indignation against those who for their personal, selfish, ambitious advantage produce this cruel deception, which destroys, not only men's bodies, but also their souls, and one feels like showing up these cruel deceivers. But the point is, that the deceivers do not deceive because they want to deceive, but because they almost cannot do otherwise. And they do not deceive in any Machiavellian way, with a consciousness of the deception which they practise, but for the most part with the naïve assurance that they are doing something good and elevated, in which opinion they are constantly maintained by the sympathy and approval of all the men who surround them. It is true that, feeling dimly that their power and their advantageous position is based on this deception, they are involuntarily drawn toward it; but they do not act because they wish to deceive the masses, but because they think that the work which they are doing is useful for the masses.

Thus emperors and kings and their ministers, performing their coronations, manœuvres, inspections, mutual visits, during which time they, dressing themselves up in all kinds of uniforms and travelling from one place to another, consult with one another with serious faces about how to pacify presumably hostile nations (who will never think of fighting with one another), are absolutely convinced that everything they do is exceedingly sensible and useful.

Similarly all the ministers, diplomatists, and all kinds of officials, who dress themselves up in their uniforms, with all kinds of ribbons and little crosses, and with preoccupation write on fine paper their obscure, twisted, useless numbered reports, communications, prescriptions, projects, are absolutely convinced that without this their activity the whole life of the nations will come to a standstill or will be entirely destroyed.

Similarly the military, who dress themselves up in their ridiculous costumes and who seriously discuss with what guns or cannon it is better to kill people, are fully convinced that their manœuvres and parades are most important and necessary for the nation.

The same conviction is held by the preachers, journalists, and writers of patriotic verses and text-books, who receive a liberal reward for preaching patriotism. Nor is any doubt concerning this harboured by the managers of celebrations, like the Franco-Russian ones, who are sincerely affected when they utter their patriotic speeches and toasts. All people do unconsciously what they do, because that is necessary, or because their whole life is based on this deception and they are unable to do anything else, while these same acts evoke the sympathy and the approval of all those men among whom they are committed. Not only do they, being all connected with one another, approve and justify the acts and the activities of one another,—the emperors and kings, the acts of the soldiers, the officials, and the clergy; and the military, the officials, and the clergy, the acts of the emperors, the kings, and one another,—the popular crowd, especially the city crowd, which sees no comprehensible meaning in everything which is being done by these men, involuntarily ascribes a special, almost a supernatural significance to them. The crowd sees, for example, that triumphal arches are being erected; that men masquerade in crowns, uniforms, vestments; that fireworks are displayed, cannon are fired, bells are rung, regiments are marching with music, documents, telegrams, and couriers fly from one place to another, and strangely masquerading men with preoccupation keep riding from one place to another, saying and writing something, and so forth,—and, not being able to verify whether there is the slightest need for what is being done (as, indeed, there is none), ascribes to all this a special, mysterious, and important meaning, and with shouts of transport or with silent awe meets all these manifestations. But in the meantime these expressions of transport and the constant respect of the crowd still more strengthen the assurance of the men who are doing all these foolish things.

Lately William II. ordered a new throne for himself, with some special ornaments, and, dressing himself up in a white uniform with patches, in tight trousers, and in a helmet with a bird on it, and throwing a red mantle over all, came out to his subjects and seated himself on this throne, with the full assurance that this was a very necessary and important act, and his subjects not only did not see anything funny in all this, but even found this spectacle to be very majestic.

XVI.

The power of the governments has now for a long time ceased to be based on force, as it was based in those times when one nationality conquered another and by force of arms held it in subjection, or when the rulers, amidst a defenceless people, maintained separate armed troops of janissaries, opríchniks, or guardsmen. The power of the governments has now for a long time been based on what is called public opinion.

There exists a public opinion that patriotism is a great moral sentiment, and that it is good and right to consider one's own nation, one's own state, the best in the world, and from this there naturally establishes itself a public opinion that it is necessary to recognize the power of the government over ourselves and to submit to it; that it is good and right to serve in the army and to submit to discipline; that it is good and right to give up our savings in the shape of taxes to the government; that it is good and right to submit to the decisions of the courts; that it is good and right to believe without verification in what is given out as a divine truth by the men of the government.

Once such a public opinion exists, there establishes itself a mighty power, which in our time has command of milliards of money, of an organized mechanism of government, the post, the telegraphs, the telephones, disciplined armies, courts, the police, a submissive clergy, the school, even the press, and this power maintains in the nations that public opinion which it needs.

The power of the governments is maintained through public opinion; but, having the power, the governments by means of all their organs, the officers of the courts, the school, the church, even the press, are always able to keep up the public opinion which they need. Public opinion produces power,—power produces public opinion. There seems to be no way out from this situation.

Thus it would, indeed, be, if public opinion were something stable and unchanging, and if the governments were able to produce the public opinion which they need.

But fortunately this is not the case, and public opinion is, in the first place, not something which is constant, unchanging, stable, but, on the contrary, something eternally changing, moving together with the motion of humanity; and, in the second, public opinion not only cannot be produced by the will of the governments, but is that which produces the governments and gives them power or takes it away from them.

It may appear that public opinion remains immovable and now is such as it was decades ago, and it may appear that public opinion wavers in relation to certain special cases, as though going back, so that, for example, it now destroys the republic, putting the monarchy in its place, and now again destroys the monarchy, putting the republic in its place; but that only seems so when we view the external manifestations of that public opinion which is artificially produced by the governments. We need only take public opinion in its relation to the whole life of men, and we shall see that public opinion, just like the time of the day or year, never stands in one place, but is always in motion, always marching unrestrictedly ahead along the path on which humanity proceeds, just as, in spite of retardations and waverings, day or spring moves on unrestrictedly along the path over which the sun travels.

Thus, though by the external signs the condition of the nations of Europe in our time is nearly the same that it was fifty years ago, the relation of the nations toward it is now entirely different from what it was fifty years ago. Though there exist, even as fifty years ago, the same rulers, armies, wars, taxes, luxury, and misery, the same Catholicism, Orthodoxy, Lutheranism, these existed before because the public opinion of the nations demanded them, but now they all exist because the governments artificially maintain that which formerly was a living public opinion.

If we frequently do not notice this motion of public opinion, as we do not notice the motion of water in the river, with the current of which we are swimming, this is due to the fact that those imperceptible changes of public opinion which form its motion are taking place in ourselves.

The property of public opinion is that of constant and unrestricted motion. If it seems to us that it is standing in one place, this is due to the fact that everywhere there are people who have established an advantageous position for themselves at a certain moment of public opinion, and so with all their strength try to maintain it and not to admit the manifestation of the new, the present public opinion which, though not yet fully expressed, is living in the consciousness of men. Such people, who retain the obsolete public opinion and conceal the new, are all those who at the present time form the governments and the ruling classes, and who profess patriotism as an indispensable condition of human life.

The means which are at the command of these people are enormous, but since public opinion is something eternally flowing and increasing, all their efforts cannot help but be vain: the old grows old, and the youthful grows.

The longer the expression of the new public opinion shall be retained, the more it will grow, and the greater will be the force with which it will express itself. The government and the ruling classes try with all their strength to retain that old public opinion of patriotism, on which their power is based, and to retard the manifestation of the new, which will destroy it. But it is possible only within certain limits to retain the old and retard the new, just as running water can be held back by a dam only within certain limits.

No matter how much the governments may try to rouse in the nations the past public opinion, now no longer characteristic of them, concerning the dignity and virtue of patriotism, the men of our time no longer believe in patriotism, but more and more believe in the solidarity and brotherhood of the nations. Patriotism now presents to men nothing but the most terrible future; but the brotherhood of the nations forms that ideal which more and more grows to be comprehensible and desirable for humanity. And so the transition of men from the former obsolete public opinion to the new must inevitably be accomplished. This transition is as inevitable as the falling of the last sere leaves in autumn and the unfolding of the young leaves in swelling buds.

The longer this transition is delayed, the more imperative does it become, and the more obvious is its necessity.

Indeed, we need only recall what it is we are professing, as Christians, and simply as men of our time, we need but recall those moral bases which guide us in our public, domestic, and private life, and that position in which we have placed ourselves in the name of patriotism, in order that we may see what degree of contradiction we have reached between our consciousness and that which among us, thanks to the intensified influence of the government in this respect, is regarded as our public opinion.

We need only reflect on those very usual demands of patriotism, which present themselves to us as something very simple and natural, in order that we may understand to what extent these demands contradict that real public opinion which we all share now. We all consider ourselves free, cultured, humane men, and even Christians, and at the same time we are in such a position that if to-morrow William takes umbrage at Alexander, or Mr. N—— writes a clever article on the Eastern question, or some prince robs the Bulgarians or the Servians, or some queen or empress takes offence at something, we all, the cultured, humane Christians, must go out to kill men, whom we do not know, and toward whom we are friendly disposed, as toward all men. If this has not yet happened, we owe this, as we are assured, to the peaceful mind of Alexander III., or to this, that Nicholas Aleksándrovich is going to marry Victoria's grandchild. But let another man be in the place of Alexander, or let Alexander himself change his mood, or Nicholas Aleksándrovich marry Amalia, and not Alice, and we shall throw ourselves like bloodthirsty animals upon one another, to take out one another's guts. Such is the supposed public opinion of our time. Such opinions are calmly repeated in all the leading and liberal organs of the press.

If we, the Christians of one thousand years' standing, have not yet cut one another's throats, it is because Alexander III. does not let us do so.

This is, indeed, terrible.

XVII.

For the greatest and most important changes to take place in the life of humanity, no exploits are needed,— neither the armament of millions of soldiers, nor the construction of new roads and machines, nor the establishment of exhibitions, nor the establishment of labour-unions, nor revolutions, nor barricades, nor explosions, nor the invention of aerial motion, and so forth, but only a change in public opinion. But for public opinion to change, no efforts of the mind are needed, nor the rejection of anything existing, nor the invention of anything unusual and new; all that is needed is, that every separate man should say what he actually thinks and feels, or at least should not say what he does not think. Let men, even a small number of them, do so, and the obsolete public opinion will fall of its own accord and there will be manifested the youthful, live, present public opinion. And let public opinion change, and the inner structure of men's life, which torments and pains them, will be changed without any effort. It is really a shame to think how little is needed for all men to be freed from all those calamities which now oppress them; they need only stop lying. Let men only not succumb to that lie which is inculcated on them, let them not say what they do not think or feel, and immediately a revolution will take place in the whole structure of our life, such as the revolutionists will not accomplish in centuries, even if all the power were in their hands.

If men only believed that the strength is not in strength, but in the truth, and if they boldly expressed it, or at least did not depart from it in words and deeds,—if they did not say what they do not think, and did not do what they consider bad and stupid.

"What harm is there in crying 'Vive la France!' or 'Hurrah!' to some emperor, king, victor, or in going in a uniform, with the chamberlain's key, to wait for him in the antechamber, to bow, and to address him by strange titles, and then to impress all young and uncultured men with the fact that this is very praiseworthy?" Or, "What harm is there in writing an article in defence of the Franco-Russian alliance or the Customs War, or in condemnation of the Germans, Russians, Frenchmen, Englishmen?" Or, "What harm is there in attending some patriotic celebration and eulogizing men whom you do not care for and have nothing to do with, and drinking their health?" Or even, "What harm is there in recognizing, in a conversation, the benefit and usefulness of treaties, or alliances, or even in keeping silent, when your nation and state is praised in your presence, and other nationalities are cursed and blackened, or when Catholicism, Orthodoxy, Lutheranism are praised, or when some war hero or ruler, like Napoleon, Peter, or the contemporary Boulanger or Skóbelev, are praised?"

All that seems so unimportant, and yet in these seemingly unimportant acts, in our aloofness from them, in our readiness to point out, according to our strength, the irrationality of what is obviously irrational,—in this does our great, invincible power consist, the power which composes that insuperable force which forms the real, actual, public opinion, which, moving itself, moves the whole of humanity. The governments know this, and tremble before this force, and with all the means at their command try to counteract it and to get possession of it.

They know that the force is not in force, but in thought and in its clear enunciation, and so they are more afraid of the expression of independent thought than of armies, and establish censorships, bribe newspapers, take possession of the management of religion and of schools. But the spiritual force which moves the world slips away from them: it is not even in a book, a newspaper,—it is intangible and always free,—it is in the depth of men's consciousness. The most powerful, intangible, freest force is the one which is manifested in man's soul, when he by himself reflects on the phenomena of the world, and then involuntarily expresses his thoughts to his wife, brother, friend, to all those men with whom he comes together, and from whom he considers it a sin to conceal what he regards as the truth. No milliards of roubles, millions of soldiers, no institutions, nor wars, nor revolutions will produce what will be produced by the simple expression of a free man as to what he considers just, independently of what exists and what is inculcated upon him.

One free man will truthfully say what he thinks and feels, amidst thousands of men, who by their acts and words affirm the very opposite. It would seem that the man who frankly expressed his thought would remain alone, while in reality it happens that all those men, or the majority of them, have long been thinking and feeling the same, but have not expressed their thought. And what yesterday was the new opinion of one man, to-day becomes the common opinion of all men. And as soon as this opinion has established itself, men's acts begin to change imperceptibly, slowly, but irresistibly.

For, as it is, every free man says to himself: "What can I do against all this sea of evil and deceit, which inundates me? Why should I give expression to my thought? Why even give form to it? It is better not to think of these obscure and intricate questions. Maybe these contradictions form an inevitable condition of all the phenomena of life. And why should I alone struggle against all this evil of the world? Would it not be better if I abandoned myself to the current which sweeps me along? If anything can be done, it can be done only in conjunction with other men."

And, abandoning that powerful instrument of thought and its expression, which moves the world, this man takes up the instrument of public activity, without noticing that all public activity is based on the very principles against which he has to struggle, that in entering upon any public activity which exists amidst our world, he must at least partially depart from the truth, make such concessions as will destroy the whole force of that powerful instrument of the struggle which is given to him. It is as though a man, into whose hands an unusually sharp dagger is given, one that cuts everything, should drive in nails with the blade.

We all deplore the senseless order of life which contradicts all our existence, and yet not only fail to make use of the one most powerful tool, which is in our hands,— the recognition of the truth and its expression,—but, on the contrary, under the pretext of struggling with evil, destroy this tool and sacrifice it to the imaginary struggle against this order.

One man does not tell the truth which he knows, because he feels himself under obligation to the men with whom he is connected; another,—because the truth might deprive him of the advantageous position by means of which he is supporting his family; a third,—because he wants to attain glory and power, to use them later in the service of men; a fourth,—because he does not wish to violate the ancient sacred traditions; a fifth,—because the expression of the truth will provoke persecution and will impair that good public activity to which he is devoting himself, or intends to devote himself.

One man serves as an emperor, king, minister, official, soldier, and assures himself and others that the deviation from the truth which is necessary in his position is more than redeemed by his usefulness.

Another exercises the office of a spiritual pastor, though in the depth of his heart he does not believe in what he teaches, permitting himself a deviation from the truth in view of the good which he does. A third instructs men in literature and, in spite of the suppression of the whole truth, in order not to provoke the government and society against himself, has no doubt as to the good which he does; a fourth simply struggles against the existing order, as do the revolutionists and anarchists, and is fully convinced that the aim which he pursues is so beneficent that the suppression of the truth, which is indispensable in his activity, and even lying will not destroy the good effect of his activity.

For the order of life which is contrary to the consciousness of men to give way to one in accord with it, it is necessary for the obsolete public opinion to give way to a live and new one.

For the old, obsolete public opinion to give way to the new, live one, it is necessary that the men who are conscious of the new demands of life should clearly express them. Meanwhile all the men who recognize all these new demands, one in the name of one thing, and another in the name of another, not only repress them, but even in words and deeds confirm what is directly opposed to these demands. Only the truth and its expression can establish that new public opinion which will change the obsolete and harmful order of life; we, however, not only do not express the truth which we know, but frequently even express precisely what we consider to be an untruth.

If free men would only not depend on what has no force and is never free,—on external power,—and would always believe in what is always powerful and free,—in the truth and its expression. If men only expressed boldly the truth, already revealed to them, about the brotherhood of all the nations and about the criminality of the exclusive membership in one nation, the dead, false public opinion, on which the whole power of the governments is based, and all the evil produced by them, would fall off by itself like a dried-up skin, and there would appear that new, live public opinion, which is only waiting for the sloughing off of the hampering old opinion, in order clearly and boldly to proclaim its demands and establish the new forms of life in accordance with the consciousness of men.

XVIII.

Men need but understand that what is given out to them as public opinion, what is maintained by such complex and artificial means, is not public opinion, but only the dead consequence of the quondam public opinion; they need only, above all, believe in themselves, in this, that what is cognized by them in the depth of their hearts, what begs for recognition and finds no expression only because it contradicts public opinion, is that force which changes the world, and the manifestation of which forms man's destiny; men need but believe that the truth is not what men about him say, but what his conscience, that is, God, says to him, and immediately there will disappear the false, artificially sustained public opinion, and the true one will be established.

If men only said what they believe, and did not say what they do not believe, there would immediately disappear the superstitions that result from patriotism, and all the evil feelings and all the violence, which are based on them. There would disappear the hatred and hostility of states against states and of nationalities against nationalities, which are fanned by the governments; there would disappear the eulogizing of military exploits, that is, of murder; there would, above all else, disappear the respect for the authorities, the surrender of people's labours and the submission to them, for which there are no foundations outside of patriotism.

Let all this be done, and immediately all that vast mass of weak men, who are always guided from without, will sweep over to the side of the new public opinion. And the new public opinion will become the ruling one in the place of the old public opinion.

Let the governments have possession of the school, the church, the press, milliards of roubles, and millions of disciplined men turned into machines,—all that apparently terrible organization of rude force is nothing in comparison with the recognition of the truth, which arises in the heart of one man who knows the force of the truth, and is communicated by this man to another, a third man, just as an endless number of candles are lighted from one. This light need only burn, and, like the wax before the face of the fire, all this seemingly so powerful organization will waste away.

If men only understood that terrible power which is given them in the word which expresses the truth. If men only did not sell their birthright for a mess of pottage. If men only made use of this power of theirs,—the rulers would not only not dare, as they dare now, to threaten men with universal slaughter, to which they will drive men or not, as they may see fit, but would not even dare in the sight of peaceable citizens to bring the disciplined murderers out on parade or in manœuvres; the governments would not dare for their own profit, for the advantage of their accomplices, to make and unmake customs treaties, and they would not dare to collect from the people those millions of roubles which they distribute to their accomplices and for which they prepare themselves for the commission of murder.

And so the change is not only possible, but it is even impossible for it not to take place, as it is impossible for an overgrown, dead tree not to rot, and for a young one not to grow. "Peace I leave with you, my peace I give unto you: not as the world giveth give I unto you; let not your heart be troubled, neither let it be afraid," said Christ. And this peace is actually already among us, and it depends on us to attain it.

If only the hearts of separate men did not grow faint from those temptations with which they are tempted every hour, and if they were not frightened by those imaginary fears with which they are terrified. If men only knew in what their mighty, all-conquering force consists, the peace for which men have always wished, not the one which is obtained by means of diplomatic treaties, journeys of emperors and kings from one city to another, dinners, speeches, fortresses, cannon, dynamite, and me-lenite, but the one which is obtained not by the exhaustion of the masses by taxes, not by tearing the flower of the population away from work and debauching them, but by the free profession of the truth by every separate individual, would long ago have come to us.

Moscow, March 17, 1894.

Printed in the USA
CPSIA information can be obtained
at www.ICGtesting.com
LVHW042156301124
798030LV00007B/269